Brilliant Rappers Educate
Intelligent Students

BREIS

Student of Life Publishing

Brilliant Rappers Educate Intelligent Students

ISBN 978-0-9568504-0-9

First published in Great Britain by Student of Life Publishing

Copyright ©Breis 2011

A Student of Life Publication

www.studentoflife.co.uk

Cover, book design and illustrations by Susan_MoreRainDesign

morerain_design@yahoo.com

Front cover illustration based on photography by Alex Winn

Identity/crest illustration based on photography by Jide Alakjia

Additional photography by Bunny Bread (Think Big), Richard Kaby (back cover)

Printed and bound in Great Britain

THE OPENING ACT

I let my mind speak before I speak my mind
Used to speak and spell now I speak divine when I speak 'n' rhyme
We can find words to uplift in an evil time; need to shine
Let the word free your mind, people I'm
Saying no need to diss or cuss but let's discuss
Plus, foul language makes your breath stink
Let no bad communication proceed out of your mouth
Only words that minister grace unto the listener
There's death and life in the power of your tongue
Create my reality with the BREIS in my lungs
Words lead to thoughts, thoughts lead to actions
Actions lead to results and reactions
So these words of mine stay positive
Never swear, just say sugar or sausages
Hope you ate 'em all
My words are pain killers you can call 'em paracetamol

Excerpt from Word Power

TURNTABLE OF LYRICAL CONTENT

TURNTABLE OF LYRICAL CONTENT

IT'S BIGGER THAN HIP HOP

I am a Master of Ceremony, half MC and half Jedi, a rap artist skilled in the art of bending sounds and words through Rhythm and Poetry. I join verses together to form a universe and blow minds with rhymes, that's why they call me BREIS (also known as Brother Reaching Each Inner Soul). Welcome to my book of rhymes and the inspiration behind them.

My love for rap music first started as a young boy living in Nigeria when I heard the female MC Roxanne Shanté. However it wasn't until years later when I returned to London that I heard a hip hop group called EPMD and really got into this exciting genre of music. I was totally captivated by the rhyming abilities and story-telling. It opened up a world full of new and strange words; I was in awe. The excitement I felt was the same feeling I wanted to give others. That's when I knew I wanted to be a rap artist. I left university with a degree in Mathematical Studies and went on to find a decent office job but my love of rhyming never stopped and I finally decided to make a career out of it.

Rapping was a way to say the things that I wasn't always able to say in my every day conversations. I could express feelings of anger, love and power even if I was too shy to do so in real life. Every line and rhyme I wrote down in my rhyme book helped me to make sense of the thoughts and feelings that lay within my mind and heart. It helped me overcome my shyness, gave me confidence and made people listen to what I had to say. I learnt how to write a verse of 16 bars with rhymes, punch lines, metaphors, similes, cultural references and wordplay.

I studied Big Daddy Kane and learnt about wit, I studied A Tribe called Quest and learnt it was OK to be myself. I studied LL Cool J and learnt about the structure of a rap song. I learnt about bravado, flow and rhyme schemes from the late Biggie Smalls; conceptual rhymes from Nas; being original from TY and standing up for something you believe in from Public Enemy. I learnt about controlling a crowd from KRS1; the importance of a good song from Blak Twang; rapping with conviction from Ghostface; lyrical content and freestyling from Common, Black Thought and Pharoahe Monch. I embraced the honesty of Lauryn Hill and putting your culture into the music from Roots Manuva. I learnt about imagination and imagery by reading books from Roald Dahl to Ben Okri. The list of influential artists goes on and on and continues even till today.

My inspiration to write comes from life; my dreams; my hopes; frustrations; conversations with friends; my faith in God; my Nigerian heritage; the streets of London; the boom bap of New York; the wisdom of my mother and grandmother. I visit hundreds of schools and colleges across the country, delivering rap workshops and performances. This book of rhymes contains some of the raps I perform and background information about each selected verse or song. Hip Hop music is more than just the foul mouthed, violent or over sexed lyrics you might be exposed to. It can be so much more. I believe my purpose is to inspire, educate and entertain people using Hip Hop as the vehicle. I hope you find the lyrics and notes in this book fun, helpful, enlightening and empowering. *Brilliant Rappers Educate Intelligent Students* and this is what I do.

Peace,

BREIS

JOURNEY

Let me take you on a journey (journey)

Follow the signs on your journey

Make sure you pack your bags early

Cos - we're going on a journey

This rap is a map you don't need a train

Boat, plane, bicycle, you just need a brain

First left, second right at the traffic lights

Keep walking straight till you come to a gate

Knock and see if **OPPORTUNITY** is in

If not – climb up **DETERMINATION** hill

Use your **SKILLS** to get you to the top

Follow the **PATIENT** path; that way you'll never drop

Now at the top of the hill eat some **HUMBLE** pie

Before your ego does something that'll make you cry

At the bottom of the hill there's an **ENVIOUS** river

To get across make sure you're holding a mirror

Called **FOCUS**, that's your protection

Everybody in life needs **DIRECTION**

Get a life, get a good **EDUCATION**

And **SUCCESS** will be your **DESTINATION**

INSPIRATION

A French Hip Hop group asked me to be on one of their tracks called JOURNEY. I immediately imagined going on the journey of life and thought of some of the signs you might see along the way. It took about half an hour to write and I was very happy with the outcome. I always wanted to do a longer version of this with more directions, dead ends, twists and turns and other interesting landmarks. This was the verse I wrote for them.

First left, second right at the traffic lights Keep walking straight till you come to a gate

When I ask someone for directions, this is the type of thing they might say even though I forget half of it before they've even finished. I try to give my raps a natural feel and include everyday phrases that people say.

MIC CHECK
See if you can draw the map of the journey rap and see what other things you could add to it. Think of goals you want to achieve and include them in your journey as destinations.

LANDMARKS AND SPENCER

Now here's a funky introduction of how nice I am

Tell your Mum, tell the Queen up in Buckingham

You can tell little women and the big men

That I rap around the clock like Big Ben

You can see what I see through my London eye

This is an avid rapid rap and not a lullaby

Breathe my lyrics in just like the O2

I'm the best at what I do cos I'm supposed to

I Tower over bridges, stay cool like fridges

I'm a Top Man like Harrods I even Sell-fridges

I spit lyrics, sharper than two swords

I make your ears stand still like Madame Tussauds

I make money like the South Bank in my raps

My mind makes movies like the IMAX

From the London Dungeon to Crystal Palaces

Nobody writes rhymes half as mad as this!

INSPIRATION

I started off with a line from one of my favourite rap artists called Phife Dawg, from the group A Tribe called Quest. The line was taken from a song called **Check the Rhime.** I twisted the ending of the second bar and from then onwards name checked as many London landmarks and shops as I could in the verse.

I spit lyrics, sharper than two swords
I make your ears stand still like Madame Tussauds

There's something exciting about rhyming with an unusual word!

MIC CHECK
How many did you spot? What other landmarks and shops can you think of?

THINK BIG

I'm crossing borderlines with broader rhymes
I generate ideas that blow your mind
You see my awesome mind does more than rhyme
I'm thinking all the time with thoughts of mine
My thoughts are 3D and HD, all combined
Sharper than the spines on a porcupine
Signed, sealed and delivery is – full of imagery
Vividly visualised through my eyes, spoken terrifically
I'm so unique; my own shadow can't even mimic me
My visions make me think into infinity
Do things differently with authenticity
And aim high specifically
Cos inside of you and inside of me
There's a place that we hide that no one can see
Do you know what you want and who you want to be?
We're bigger than we think but it's hard to see

Fling your mind to the edge of the world… now bring it back
Think outside the box and in your thinking cap
Dream bigger than you think your dreams can be
Open up your mind's eye so it can see
Possible impossibilities

Unlimited things to achieve so don't be limited
Or prohibited from getting into it
My intuition is telling me your ambition is big
Don't let people get you mad, get even
Always think big and believe in
Your ability to do things you thought you couldn't
You might think that you can't, but really you shouldn't
Cos inside of you and inside of me
There's a genius inside that no one can see
Do you know what you want and who you want to be?
We're bigger than we think but it's hard to see

On the positive things place your emphasis
To neutralise the negative blemishes
Ever since my youth I knew that I was meant for this
Sent with this to help you fly like Pegasus
You might blame others for your bad sentences
But sometimes we're our own arch nemesis
In the crevices of your premises, the premise is
Achieving greatness is your genesis

INSPIRATION

It was the summer of 2004 and I had just finished touring with a Cuban jazz band. During this period I had time to catch up on some reading and started thinking of other things to do in my spare time. All these amazing ideas started to come to me and I suddenly realised that I could do a lot more things in life, simply because I gave myself the time to think about them. I wrote this song to remind myself and everyone that we can accomplish so much more when we allow our minds to think big. Every time I think I'm not capable of doing something, this song reminds me that I can.

I'm so unique; my own shadow can't even mimic me
My visions make me think into infinity

The line about the shadow is fun because it's a brilliant exaggeration of the point I'm making about being unique. As an MC it's all about being original with words and expressions. The second bar is saying it's important to have a vision because it stops you from being limited in life.

MIC CHECK
What awesome thing will you do or create to make life better for your family, friends, town, country or world?

CAPTAIN OF THE SHIP

I'm the Captain of ship, master of the mast
I've had my left hand chopped off in the past
That's why they call me Captain Hook
You can see me on the cover of your favourite book
I'm a top deck chilling, ruthless villain
In my galleon I'm making a killing
I'm courageous, fearless and brave
My cutlass sends other pirates to their grave
I sail the seas with a crew that serve me
Bristles in my beard and a mouth full of scurvy
I can hold a whole ship to ransom
I've lost three teeth but I'm still quite handsome
Shiver me timbers, shivers down your spine
If you spot a Jolly Roger it might be mine
Prisoners walk the plank before we dine
That shiny compass is mine, mine, mine!

Anchors away, cabin boys do the rigging

We're off to find treasure, spades for the digging

A flying jib is on my ship, it's a beauty

To be the wickedest pirate is my duty

We call our ship the Dungeon Dragon

Other ships feel the BOOM from the cannon!

Arr, Arr, what will we see?

When we travel across land and sea

INSPIRATION

A teacher asked if I could help her write a rap for her seven year old students. The whole class wanted to recite a rap about pirates, so I came up with this. He's one of the scariest pirates I've ever known!

I've lost three teeth, but I'm still quite handsome

This captain still thinks he's handsome with his mouth full of scurvy and missing teeth, love it!

MIC CHECK
Don't forget, you are the captain of your ship.
Be courageous, be brave, but most importantly
keep your teeth clean!

WAHALA

Pidgin English

Weytin dey happen for dis world where we dey?

Wàhálà just dey come like *wéré, wéré*

Some people want make wàhálà come find dem

Me? I just dey mind my own *jéjé, jéjé*

We want better we no want suffer

Life is hard enough, why make things tougher?

Problems dey everywhere, no escapism

Go for overseas you go see racism

Crime and poverty, corrupt sociology

Volatile economy, unemployment-ology

Hi-technology, nothing works properly

Lord deliver me, lead make I follow thee

Plan one thing, *na* another thing *selè*

You never plan for dat one *télè, télè*

Kíló selè? The stress, palaver

Everyone I know has to deal with *wàhálà*

Interpretation

What's happening in this world that we live in?
Trouble keeps coming really quickly
Some people want trouble to come and find them
As for me, I just mind my own business peacefully
We want a better life we don't want to suffer
Life is hard enough, why make things tougher?
Problems are everywhere, no escaping that
If you go overseas, you'll see racism
Crime and poverty, a corrupt society
Volatile economy, unemployment
Hi-technology, nothing works properly
Lord deliver me, lead and let me follow you
Plan one thing, and another thing happens
You never planned for that before
What's the matter? The stress, palaver
Everyone I know has to deal with trouble

INSPIRATION

Pidgin English is a language spoken in various parts of West Africa like Sierra Leone, Nigeria, Ghana and Cameroon. Creole (using French instead of English) and West Indian Patois are similar types of languages. I learnt how to speak Pidgin English and Yoruba when I lived in Nigeria as a young boy and still use it to speak to some of my family and friends today. I had never heard of rap in Pidgin English when I wrote my first Pidgin rap but today many Nigerian rappers rap in Pidgin and their own Nigerian language (e.g. Yoruba, Igbo). Wahala is a Yoruba word meaning trouble. For example, a parent might tell their misbehaving child, "Stop giving me wahala!"

Volatile economy, unemploymentology

I made up a new word here. Unemploymentology is the study of unemployment.

YOUR FAVOURITE EMCEE

Who's your favourite emcee, rapper or lyricist?
Street-poet, story teller, griot or wordsmith?
Whose tracks do you rewind? Whose lyrics do you quote?
Whose flow is so flawless? Who always gets your vote?
For president, prevalence, sounding intelligent?
Excellence and elegance and eloquence is evident
In this time of decadence, still sounds relevant
Squashing sucker MCs like an angry elephant

Are they *Special like Ed?* Freestyle from the head?
Old or new school? When they move a crowd it's kind of dread?
Whose lyrical content and voice do you like?
Who uses tears as ink so you can feel what they write?
Are they original, solo or in a collective?
Unknown, simply complex or introspective?
Did you learn something old from a new perspective?
What's their objective? Who's your favourite MC?

INSPIRATION

Rap music started in New York in the early '70s, but rap can be traced back to Jamaica, where the rappers were called DJs. Going further back, rap is similar to the oral traditions of the griots of Western Africa who have been around for centuries. Griots are historians, praise singers, verbal keepers of knowledge and information of their people. "Who's the best MC, Master of Ceremony?" Is a popular question that's always asked. The answers are not based on good looks, how much money they make or whether they're in the charts; it's strictly based on their skills, originality, flow, voice and impact of their songs etc. When I started emceeing I wanted to be the best, but later on realised that being the best was just an illusion. Writing meaningful songs that inspire and educate people became my new goal.

Are they Special like Ed? Freestyle from the head?

Special Ed is one of my favourite old school MCs. Freestyling is a skill any good MC should possess. It's the ability to make up rhymes on the spot that have never been written before. It takes imagination, knowledge and speed of thought to pull off a good freestyle (plus freestyles come in handy if you forget your lyrics on stage).

MIC CHECK
Who's your favourite MC and why?

27

PUSH CHORUS

Don't give up, you've got to push

You're almost there so just push

Everybody needs a push

So have some faith and just push

INSPIRATION

PUSH is all about not giving up. You might feel like giving up sometimes but if you just push a little harder, you'll get to the finish line. My younger sister told me she used to play this song everyday whilst she was studying hard at University. It helped her get through months of late night studying. PUSH could also stand for Pray Until Something Happens.

Everybody needs a push

Sometimes you need encouragement from others to know that you're capable of doing something. Sometimes you have to encourage others to do great things too. Everybody needs a helping hand from time to time.

MIC CHECK
Can you remember the last time you felt like giving up but didn't? How good did it feel that you pushed through? Remember that feeling the next time you feel like giving up.

NO CONDITION IS PERMANENT

Life changes like the weather
Whether windy or cold
Snowflakes or sunny spells
Or what the weatherman told
Old was once new, the youth age things change
It's strange when things in your range rearrange
Moments we live become memories
As time advances
We all go through impenetrable circumstances
And dance with wolves
I light a candle burn a scent
Remember when my Granny said
NO CONDITION IS PERMANENT

It's hard to earn a cent
Let alone a pound is what I found
When my CV is on the ground
And my sound is underground
But I never lost heart
I hung onto these words that BREIS heard
Walked in the knowledge
Until my knees hurt
As Earth revolves birth evolves and folds
Into the future she holds, which
Involves all the problems we solve
Change occurs with time in divine order
Or whenever it's clever only eternity lasts forever

INSPIRATION

"No condition is permanent", was a phrase I heard my Grandmother use back in Nigeria. It always stuck with me and reminded me that anytime things were going horribly wrong, it wouldn't always be that way. Eventually things would have to change. It was inevitable. Likewise when things are going great and life is like chocolate, things can suddenly go wrong. So enjoy the good times when they're here but prepare for the bad times too. That way when the not so good times arrive, they won't be so hard to deal with.

Remember when my Granny said NO CONDITION IS PERMANENT

I'm proud of the fact that I did a rap that included my Grandmother.
I don't know many rappers that have done that before. LoL.

MIC CHECK
What piece of advice have you heard that has really helped you?

COLOURFUL RETURN

In my dream I'm in the back room of my flat's womb

Hear a rap tune as I look upon a black moon

Back soon I said, that soon?

In two years at noon

To croon from rap sheets, writing blue notes on black beats

Back streets stealing my magnolia

Holier than black skin in red clothes, in dey go

To tell me I'm too golden for this yellow show

Telling me pink fibs but their lie lack (lilac) passion

Eyes lack compassion, I cry purple rain

Staining orange grass for miles of green miles

I've seen smiles of beige white teeth

I've come a long way, from running after rainbows

And witches tryna kill me from birth

You live and you learn

Ultra-violet, pilot my return!

INSPIRATION

This verse was inspired by an extremely vivid dream I once had. It was full of rich colours and was also very mystical. When I started writing this piece, I connected some of the colours to titles of films, songs and books. See if you can spot any. There is a mixture of reality and fantasy in this rap. It's also telling a story.

Staining orange grass for miles of green miles I've come a long way, from running after rainbows

The image of orange grass is very strong and very strange. The second line is something that happened in real life when I was really little.

MIC CHECK
Imagine everything in the world was a totally different colour to what it is now.

BIRDS ON A TREE

Birds on a tree, birds on a tree

Tweet, tweet, tweet, birds on a tree

Into the woods and what do I see?

I see twenty birds perched on a tree

Twenty birds in Mother Nature's class

A hunter walks past on the soft grass

Holding a rifle, he aims higher

Spots one of the birds, aim, fire!

He shoots one bird and it falls to the ground

The sound of chaos is heard all around

How many birds will be left on the tree?

When you get the right answer come and find me

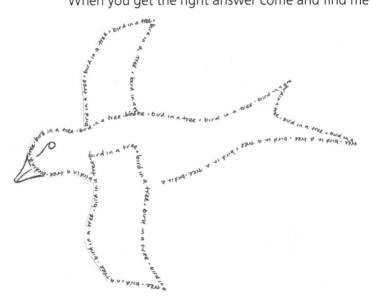

INSPIRATION

This is a riddle I heard years ago. I loved it so much and decided to turn it into a short rap. Did you get the correct answer? You might have to close your eyes and imagine it line for line and the correct answer will present itself.

I see twenty birds perched on a tree

This is the first time I've been able to use the word perched in a rap verse! It's not really an unusual word; I've just never had an opportunity to use it in a rap before.

MIC CHECK
Are there any words you can't imagine being used in a rap? Or know of words that can't be rhymed with? By the way, I can rhyme with the word orange!

2012

Two thousand and twelve, two thousand and twelve
Olympic Games in two thousand and twelve
Colourful flags from many a country
Sports from weight lifting to archery
Athletes compete with their hands and their feet
No surrender and no defeat
Shooting for the stars let's keep on winning
A beautiful sight like synchronised swimming
The whole world's looking at the London Eye
London city making Olympics fly
The village is bonkers! The streets are fizzy
So much traffic your eyes go dizzy
Will I be in East London or watch from home?
Athletes from Paris, Nairobi and Rome
It might be nice to see the athletes in person
I just hope the athletes have started rehearsing

INSPIRATION

The Olympic Games takes over any city it visits and London is
no exception. I thought of what London might be like during this
period with so many different nationalities all around, soaking up
the atmosphere.

Will I be in East London or watch from home?

I'll have to wait and see.

MIC CHECK
What are you a champion at doing?

JAMMIN ON THE BUS

Mans was jamming, jamming on the bus
There were one, two, three, about four of us
You dun know *fam*, we love to chat
We can chat for England and that's a fact
Voices come like amplified speakers
Words are missiles with the heat seekers
"Reh, reh, reh", this girl's chatting her business
For everybody on the top deck to witness
But don't watch that, I'm watching an old man
Sleeping and dribbling on somebody's gran
We didn't want to, but we laughed when we looked
The old man woke up, gave us an evil look
Music from our phone makes us act merry
Erickson, Nokia, iPhone and Blackberry
Bare tunes on my mp3
Talib Kweli, Tinie (Tempah), Ty and Wiley

I'm a DJ, the bus is my club
But these passengers don't show me any love
Even adults are scared to go up above
Then I heard one girl call another girl *"bruv"*
I turned my head, anti-clockwise
My eyes realised that they were not guys
Four girls all louder than us
All cussing and causing a fuss
I saw one passenger leave in a rush
The look on her face was of pure disgust
One girl was giving another girl grief
Then I heard her say, "I'll knock out your teeth"
The driver stopped the bus to provide relief
The whole episode was beyond belief
It was all quite negative and not a plus
Just another day when you're jamming on the bus

INSPIRATION

Many times on my way to perform in a school or after a long day of workshops, I've had the pleasure of taking a bus ride with school children. Let's just say I've heard many things from the mouths of both boys and girls that cannot even be repeated in this book. I won't be surprised if in the future there has to be a referee on the top deck of some London buses. This was just a mild snapshot of the atmosphere and youthful language you might get on any given day. (It's not always this bad though). Slang has always been a big part of rapping, in a way it's a whole new coded language *(slanguage)*.

I'm a DJ, the bus is my club

There was a time when mobile mp3 players were being used like ghetto blasters. That was the worst! At least most people use headphones now, but even some headphones leak out so much sound that it can sometimes feel like you're at a rave with bad sound systems playing different tunes!

MIC CHECK
Do you use slanguage to communicate?

IDENTITY

Heavenly sent to me so it was meant to be

I'm already mentally who I'm meant to be eventually

They couldn't see this entity's intensity immensity

Didn't invest in me, but that wasn't my destiny

Don't mess with me, God given energy

To crush my enemy like a centipede, but I'm friendly

At ten to three, secret assignment is to MC

I'll do it for free but first pay my rent for me

I'm ebony and every-body's telling me

How to be, I won't let it be a dent in me

Let me be me, the best in me is yet to be

Don't need an ID card to show you my identity

In a class of my own I tend to be essentially

A student of life, it's elementary

Not me, but a conduit I get to be

The Word in me is next to me

This world is full of lies, everybody's in a guise

Despise and diss guys in disguise that spit lies

A bit wise behind my eyes and behind my disguise

I'm a fat guy mistaking MCs for mince pies

Throw your hands in the air, reach for the skies

I rise till I realise: I am the prize

But don't be surprised when I enter-prise

I'm blessed, I'm a blessing, I'm a blessing in disguise

Disguised in a body – soul, spirit

My whole lyric - no limit, so go get it

Why did he do it? Cos flows are good for his health

Bona fide Rhymes Exist In Self

For my life I thank God, *Olúwaseun*

When I'm feeling hungry, I'm like *mo fé jeun*

MCs or *àkàrà, wò ó* no time for *sakará*

I'm blacker than an adder in an *agbádá*

MCs think they're badder, scatter *pátápátá*

Snakes get sadder cos I climb up the ladder

That's why I take the pee like a bladder

You can call me *de don dada or bàbá Àlí bàbá*

Open sesame seed buns for chicken burgers

Run and tell your mama or your papa – I'm a rapper

Hakuna matata – everything's kriss, what's the matter?

You can't take it then step like *bàtà*

Oh *chale*, he just flows like ballet

Showing you a new style, please don't *jalè*

That means don't steal, this is how I keep it real

My people in the place tell me how you feel

KEY

Yoruba words

Olúwaseun – thank you God

mo fé jeun – I want to eat

àkàrà – Is a Nigerian snack made from beans, grounded, seasoned and fried... A fried bean cake

Sakará – showing off

agbádá – A traditional Nigerian outfit for men

pátápátá – completely

bàtà – shoes

jalè – steal

bàbá Àlí bàbá – the father of Ali Baba (meaning even wiser than Ali Baba)

Other languages and slang terms

Hakuna matata –Swahili for no worries

Chale – Ghanian expression used in many ways. In this case, it means *"my friend"*

De don dada – the top player/ the best

Everything's kriss – everything is fine

INSPIRATION

The first verse started off as a freestyle. I wanted to continue rhyming with Identity with as many words/phrases for as long as possible. The second verse was all about wordplay and exploring different disguises. The third verse actually came first. It was the first verse I had ever written in English and Yoruba and had written it about four years earlier. It was originally meant to be for a song called African necklace that I wanted to record with other MCs from different African countries. I never got around to doing it but thought it would work perfectly at the end of this song.

It's the B to the, the R to the, the E to the I, to the S and I'm an African disguised as a Westerner. These are the lead lines from the chorus. The main aim was to educate people on how to spell my name correctly. The second line acknowledges the two different cultures I was raised in. For a long time, I only viewed myself as being African and not British. As an adult I now appreciate and accept that I am both.

Heavenly sent to me so it was meant to be I'm already mentally who I'm meant to be eventually

The whole of the third verse is my most treasured verse to date but outside of that I love these two lines. They started the whole song off with a philosophical thought and six rhymes in a rhyming couplet. That's Big! B.R.E.I.S stands for many things (see the end of verse two for one of them).

MIC CHECK
See if you can create a new meaning to your name eg Raj could stand for Reliable And Jovial. Make sure the meaning of your name matches either your personality or what you do.

TIP: You can use a dictionary for help.

RIGHT HERE IN FRONT OF YOU

We deliver gems from the river Thames to the river Nile

With a smile, *E jé kín báayín sòrò* for a while

BREIS electrify, TY intensify

Putting sleep to sleep like a tsetse fly

Let me stretch the sky etch my eye

In your vision with precision when I testify

The Heroes in the song Unsung by the gallon

Breis, raised on the drums of Tony Allen

Na so e be when you check the way I set am

Spies falling from skies self, *no go get am*

Mummy travelled over 3,000 miles

To turn 3,000 tears into 3,000 smiles

3,000 files of family and friends

Invited to dinner so I happily attend

And then I send this one to my people back home

It's Breis on the microphone

KEY

Yoruba

E jé kín báayín sòrò = let me talk to you

Pidgin English

Na so e be when you check the way I set am Spies falling from skies self, no go get am = That's how it is when you check the way I did it. Even spies falling from skies wouldn't get it

INSPIRATION

This verse is from a track called *Right here in front of you*
produced by Unsung Heroes and is featured on *The Rough Guide
to African Rap* album. The drums on this track were played by the
legendary Tony Allen who alongside Fela Kuti created the Afro
beat rhythms. One of the UK's finest rappers, Ty asked if I wanted
to join him on the track and I jumped at the opportunity. It was
an honour to be part of such a project and remains one of the
highlights of my musical career. In this verse I made sure I
name checked all the artists involved.

We deliver gems from the river Thames to the river Nile
With a smile, E jé kin báayin sóró for a while

These opening lines sum up what the whole verse is about. Delivering 'gems' or brilliant rhymes are what every good MC wants to do. At home when we're speaking to each other as a family we love mixing in Yoruba words and phrases in English sentences. I wanted to reflect that practice in my lyrics and give it an authentic feel. I also added some *Pidgin English.*

MIC CHECK
Did you ever speak a made up language when you were younger? My younger sisters used to speak what they called *bobo* language.
Ibit wabos habord tobo sabay = it was hard to say

ONLY HUMAN

I wasn't raised with a silver spoon more like a wooden one

Nuff beatings on my bum, considered really troublesome

But I was just a bubblegum, young glum troubled one

Tryna be a child in the hood of adulthood

I'd study for days to get As. Be pleased to see Bs

Found music found Nuff CDs

If these teachers can't teach, I can't learn

In turn I burn the midnight oil and let the candle burn

Now the roof, the roof, the roof is on fire!

Step daddy's gonna kill me like a hit man for hire

Picture mummy screaming ten seconds after dreaming

The flames on my hair leaving smoke on the ceiling

Rescue my sisters, quench the fire; face the music

When nothing I do is good enough I fine tune it

Before I lose it, like my balance when I'm skiing

You're seeing super emceeing from a special human being

It's hard being a hue man; I'm only human
In a cruel world's television show I'm a Truman
Kool and the gang when I hang up my hang ups
It's Breis on the banger hang my anger on a hanger
They can't see the venom in him they just know his pen is illin
Lyrically healing the world more than penicillin
But when dealing with a mind from where I'm from
It's like a bygone time bomb in Saigon
Ladies want Mr. Right, I'm on a leftfield
Not perfect but I'm worth it is how I heard it
And if I have to tell you to respect this guy
You must be blind in your ear and deaf in your eye
I did what I didn't want to do when I did it
Didn't do what I should've when I could've I admit it
But God gave me grace put a smile on my face
Humans are fragile in this human race

INSPIRATION

When I was younger, it felt as if my parents never understood me and I could never do anything right. I got into trouble quite a bit but made sure I never did anything so bad that it would bring shame to my mum. I learnt that you can't please everybody all the time whether its parents, teachers or friends and as humans we all make mistakes in life. The trick is to learn the lesson after you've made a mistake so you don't repeat it. This song starts off in autobiographical style, capturing the imperfections and mental struggles we face as human beings. It ends on a note of hope that even though this human being goes through all this madness, the grace of God gives him peace and joy.

You must be blind in your ear and deaf in your eye

This was just an original way of saying "it doesn't make sense".
I call this a bit of a brain twister.

MIC CHECK
So you're only human, however what if you could be a super human, what powers would you have and what would your main mission be?

SEPARATION

Separated from my heart so I'm heartless

I despise everyone regardless

Why should my life have to be the hardest?

What did I ever do to start this?

Was it sin that brought this trouble I'm in?

I lost yesterday but tomorrow I'll win

One day happiness and I will meet

Like the ground and the soles of my feet

INSPIRATION

This was written as part of a play I wrote called *Ife* (which means love in Yoruba). It was a musical that used rap, drama, music and dance to tell a love story of a husband and wife who became separated. This was one of the raps by the husband.

Why should my life have to be the hardest?

I think this is a question we all ask ourselves at some point in life when we think everything in our world is going against us.

MIC CHECK
Do you look forward to being reunited with something you've been separated from?

plough

vow

bow

dhow

ciao

brow

row

how

I knew a young MC with more beef than a _____

Itchy finger ready with the *braaap and blow*

Raised on music that raised his eye _____

Made him say _____ I wonder _____

I can be a *badman* like that right _____

Started practicing over that rhythm called _____

Went to a rave in the middle of _____

When people see me I'm gonna make them _____

Clashing crews in twos then got into a _____

"Take man for a joke man I'll show them _____

Badman dig a hole into you like a _____

He did the evil do and sailed off like a _____

Little did he know that the crew made a _____

To _____ any who treat like man like _____

He got his wish when everyone said _____

And the Rev (Reverend) said, "Close your eyes and please _____"

now

wow

Slough

meow

chow

Pow!

how

cow

bow

INSPIRATION

There is a Proverb that says, "Death and life are in the power of the tongue, and those that love it will eat its fruit." (Proverbs 18:21) which means be careful of the words you use because you might get exactly what you say. That is what this fictional story is about. I've come across young MCs that wanna clash/battle other crews or MCs but instead of keeping the battle lyrical, it gets out of hand and spills in to real life violence. This story is told in a very light manner even though it's dealing with themes of death and violence. Battling and story-telling have always been key in raps. Artists like Slick Rick, Biggie Smalls, Nas, Outkast, Sway etc do it well. This verse is also inspired partly by a rapper called Doug E Fresh (amazing beat boxer also). In one of his performances, he encouraged the audience to fill in the missing words to his verse. When I perform this verse I do the same thing.

When people see me I'm gonna make them bow...

And the Rev (Reverend) said, "Close your eyes and please bow"

These two lines tell the whole story. The young man got what he said he wanted, just not how he had imagined it. The Reverend is a clue to where he was when he got his wish.

 MIC CHECK
Fill in the gaps by choosing the correct word to complete each sentence.

THE CHEMISTRY

We're like H_2O, I'm oxygen you're my Hydrogen

Your mind and soul is where my mind is in

It's chemistry when we gel like sap from a tree

There's love and trust so with you, I'm free

They say communication is the key

I'll be open with you, you be open with me

No need to point fingers that is pointless

We say how we feel cos we're far from voiceless

You put me in my place when I'm acting under par

And you're very supportive, your knowledge goes far

I give you space cos you're a star

And every time I see you I'm like *uh uh ar!*

I'm the head and you're the neck

Protect your neck, show it love and respect

With kisses and perfume don't let it feel neglect

Or you might end up with a pain in the neck

INSPIRATION

What makes two people that like each other get on so well? There are many answers like trust, admiration and respect. I wrote this to explore some of those things and being a bit of a science geek, I wanted to sprinkle a few scientific terms over it too.

I'm the head and you're the neck

Protect your neck, show it love and respect

I heard the first line from an older relative when I was younger and always found the theory fascinating. *Protect your neck* is also a reference to one of Hip Hop's most strategic groups, Wu Tang Clan.

MIC CHECK
What are the top five things that make a great friendship or relationship?

STRICTLY

See how the Breis flows to tha

Beats that go through a Yoruba native son

Speak my mother tongue plus in a native tongue

Over the *sekere*, loop or my native drum

The oral lore passed down from an ancient one

So move your body whether *small pikin* or eighty one

Defending it, even after the plaintiff's done

One of the nicest MCs, I'm a blatant one

Afro beats and Afri – lyrics is your acquisition

Of Afro vision on admission had to add the mission

Respect tradition and I love my culture, love my heritage

But every where I turn, (it's) depicted as negative

I never give into the media's selective sedative

This one's for you if you're a fan, friend or relative

Imperative you come nearer, my mission's clearer

Cos your mind is like skin and I'm like aloe vera

Your unremitting resistance against my existence

Induces my persistence, insistence for instance

I make my words go the distance

From man on road to impressionable infants

And use the beat for assistance

My identity and me in co-existence

The sun shines and winds rush together

Hope they get along, can't always blame snow for rainy weather

Strictly for my people feeling cold in town

That hold a frown, but really they just hold it down

For heroes we never see but ubiquitous

Ridiculous, how they remain inconspicuous

I write tunes for mums who lost sons to knife wounds

And when the night wounds daughter's of life's womb

Home or away tryna make ends meet

This is strictly for my, strictly for my, strictly for my peeps

KEY

Sekere – a Yoruba word for a percussive shaker
Small pikin – Pidgin English for small child
Afri – lyrics – African centred lyrics

INSPIRATION

As a young man growing up in London, I noticed a lot of negativity towards many people of African descent especially from the media. I wrote STRICTLY to highlight how I felt about this and to say that if my presence and contributions were ignored by society, it would only force me to achieve even more. This was also to acknowledge people like my mum who work extremely hard within society but go unseen or unheard. I've always been proud of my Nigerian heritage and encourage students to be proud of where they're from. Whether Portuguese, Somali, Pakistani or Polish, be proud of where you're from and represent your culture in the right way, whilst respecting other people's cultures.

Cos your mind is like skin and I'm like aloe vera
The sun shines and winds rush together

This is one of my favourite punch lines. The second line has a play on words and meaning.

DON'T FOREVER HOLD YOUR PEACE

Not a word, not a peep, not a squeak just silence

Lonely hearts need LOL and guidance

Screams evaporate into silent sirens

It's a different type of domestic violence

Phones on silent, weak reception

With a good network but no connection

Feeling guilty, so much shame

I can tell by how you're looking you've never felt the same

It's harder today cos it's harder to pray

My self control finds it harder to stay

I don't want your pity I just wanna be whole

Listen to me closely and hug my soul

I'm trying to keep quiet but it's too much to bear

What will you think of me if I dare to share?

If I share my thoughts in your court will you judge me?

I'm scared to speak cos I still want you to love me
Don't wanna be the disappointment appointment
And make things slippery like ointment
The truth will set you free, said the listener
But I feel safer as a prisoner
I don't wanna have to explain myself
I'm all on my own tryna change myself
I need to let these feelings out as I speak out
But if you're listening please don't freak out

INSPIRATION

Bottling up strong emotions and not letting them out can do serious damage to you. Some people get rid of their frustration and anger through dancing, playing sports, singing, rapping, writing or simply talking to a true friend. Whether it's about trouble at home, bullying, not being treated fairly, find someone you can trust and SPEAK to them. It might be a parent, brother, sister or a professional but speak out and get the right help. Someone very close to me showed me the importance of this and inspired me to write this.

If I share my thoughts in your court will you judge me?

I'm scared to speak cos I still want you to love me

I like the word association between being judged and a court, where judges judge from. Both lines show reasons that might hold us back from speaking out.

MIC CHECK
How do you get rid of anger and frustration in a sensible way?

FEAR OF FAILURE

Fear of rejection, fear of being wrong

Fear of a black planet, fear of moving on

...Fear of change, fear of the unknown

Fear of fear, fear of being all alone

...Fear of success, fear of failure

God gave me talent but look at my behaviour

Brake, clutch, change gear; I make a beat melt

And then I hold myself back like a seatbelt

When everyone is running I'm doing the running man

I should be further ahead, I don't understand

I'm not where I wanna be, feeling like a wannabe

I wanna be where my destiny really wanted me

Even if what I wanna be isn't all it's ought to be

Start recording me before I get disorderly

Tryna be perfect leads to procrastination

I heard failure is future information

Never believe False Evidence Appearing Real
Face the fear and do it anyway is how I feel
If I fail I fail, if I win I win
Let me finish, let me persevere but let me begin
The Prayer eaters, Love haters and Nay Sayers
Dream delayers, Doubt bringers and Passion killers
They wanna kill us and fill us with fear
But there's only love, power and a sound mind here
Every time you find fear tell him bye bye dear
Don't bother bring your stagnant self around here
Mummy said go for it, this is my year
African Shakespeare; big things for my career
It's clear - we need some more faith in here
Put yourself out there in the atmosphere
Fear only attracts what you're afraid of
So let your light shine and show them what you're made of

INSPIRATION

FEAR stands for False Evidence Appearing Real. There is a type of fear that is a warning and should be listened to. Like if I see a big dirty hungry-looking dog growling at me and I feel fear, it makes sense to listen to that fear. However if I feel fearful about something that hasn't happened and more importantly probably won't, then that fear is really just an illusion my mind is creating and shouldn't be listened to. I wrote this once I realised that the intention of fear was to stop us from moving on with our lives.

Fear only attracts what you're afraid of So let your light shine and show them what you're made of

These lines sum up the whole song.

MIC CHECK
Make a list of things you're afraid of and see if they're a warning or an illusion.

SHARON

Nine o'clock one morning, just the other day

Before I woke up and even had a chance to pray

Was awoken by a phone call

(I said) go away

Turned out to be a friend with something to say

"I'm so upset so much hurt today

She's still alive but her life's been taken away"

I'm like, "Who?"

"Sharon, met her a while back, she had a smile that

Made you wanna smile back

But behind her smile, a broken heart

Broken bones down the stairs of a broken home

Physical, verbal abuse, stolen identity

She had to flee from the hand of the enemy"

How evil is the evil in man?

We come against the enemy's plan

Fear no man and wipe away your tears

Beautiful woman stay strong and hold on

Like an island nobody knows
And in your summertime sometimes it snows
Nobody to talk to, no one to help
Life's forced you to do everything yourself
You've been through so much; you don't know how to cope
Your baby girl looks up to you for hope
And the problems that you're facing won't just disappear
But I want to make something crystal clear
Hearing about you makes me humble
To be where you are and know you didn't crumble
You're gonna get through this cos God loves you so
You're gonna look back and think *"man, that was horrible!*
But now I'm doing better in a better place
And happiness is shinning on my face
My past can't hurt me anymore
Cos my future is a bright open door"

INSPIRATION

As a young man I was told never raise your hand to hit a girl. As a man, that was one of the weakest and most disgraceful things you could ever do. It's really sad how many young ladies have been victims of domestic violence. And in some cases men have been victims also.

I wrote this rap song on my birthday after receiving a phone call and hearing about this woman's unfortunate circumstances. I wrote this for her and for any woman or child that has been the victim of physical, verbal and emotional abuse. My prayer is that one day they escape the madness they're in and have the chance to rebuild their life again. Wherever you are Sharon I wish you well.

Like an island nobody knows And in your summertime sometimes it snows

This highlights the loneliness and abandonment she feels. The second line paints a picture of something that shouldn't naturally happen. Neither should domestic violence.

MIC CHECK
Can you think of other strange things that shouldn't naturally happen?

FINANCIAL ADVISER

My bud said get wiser invest in an ISA

Instead of spending all your money tryna look nicer

Write a bit tighter to be a rich writer

The galaxy's guide for every hitch hiker

It's like a light bulb on your head shining brighter

I went to see a Financial Adviser

His name was Elijah from Naija, chief like Kaiser

Supervisor with an organiser

Looking like a biker he parked his Micra

Listened to my story, then he said,

"I like ya. I can tell your money needs some moisturiser

Cos you keep spending money with the eye of the tiger"

I get the point like a hyper sniper

But can you make money follow me like the piper?

"I'll show you how to get rich and not be a miser

I can make your money stretch like Lycra

Give 10 percent to God first, become a tither

That's why He turns my 50 pence into a fiver

Then 20 percent's for you to save and invest

The rest – for you to live on and pay off your debts

Never spend more than what you're left with

Think rich – make money come to your senses

Increase your earnings, save your pences

Stop buying things you don't need cut your expenses"

I found my adviser a bit offensive

He looked me in the eye and said,

"Don't get defensive"

About defensive! Are you defective?

I didn't come here to be disrespected!

"I'm a millionaire and my style's expensive

Stop being a consumer, start being inventive

I'm sorry, I'm not tryna be funny

But would you ask broke people how to make money?"

INSPIRATION

I've never been the type of rapper that raps about how incredibly broke I am or how ridiculously rich I am either. I just wanted to write about money from a more realistic and ordinary point of view. So I imagined someone like myself seeking financial advice and turned it into a dialogue between myself and the financial adviser.

Write a bit tighter to be a rich writer
The galaxy's guide for every hitch hiker

The Hitch Hiker's Guide to the Galaxy was one of my favourite books. I like including personal and cultural references in my raps and was happy to play around with the title to fit the rap.

MIC CHECK
A lot of research went into this and there really is a lot of practical advice in this verse. Follow it and watch how rich you become. Terms and conditions apply.

INTERLUDE

To follow BREIS' music, visit his blog **www.breismusic.wordpress.com**

When Breis isn't recording music or touring, he delivers Hip Hop and performance poetry workshops to hundreds of schools and colleges (ages 7 and upwards). He encourages young people to take an interest in Literacy through the medium of rap music and helps bring out their creativity. He also carries out INSET training sessions with teachers on creativity in the classroom.

"The workshops were inspirational and fun! BREIS created an environment where students were learning without even realising it and were able to express themselves freely"

Zehra Jaffer, Assistant Head teacher, Wallington County Grammar School

TEACHERS

You can book BREIS to perform some of his work or facilitate workshops by visiting www.studentoflife.co.uk or emailing him directly at
studentoflife.ltd@gmail.com

To find out more about Student of Life, visit **www.studentoflife.co.uk** or
www.iamstudentoflife.blogspot.com

The correct answer to the question on page 37 is zero because all the other birds fly away.

CALL AND RESPONSE

Thank you for purchasing a copy of Brilliant Rappers Educate Intelligent Students. By buying this book you have also supported the children's charity BBSI (Bless, Break & Share It Trust Ltd). They're a small charity doing big things. They are presently working on their orphanage in Kenya in order to house more desperate children living in slum regions. Student of Life will be giving a portion of the proceeds from this book to BBSI.

You can find out more at **www.bbsi-trust.org**

Help us by telling your friends, teachers or students about this book. Tweet about it, put it on Facebook, YouTube it, dosomethingoranything dot com to get the word out about it.

Student of Life is also connected to a brilliant organisation called Find Your Voice. They encourage people to express themselves in a creative manner, by making handmade postcards and taking part in fun activities. Find your voice wants everyone to know that their life means something in society. By taking part in the variety of projects, they hope to unleash the creative side of people and a desire to make communities a more exciting place.

Check them out on **www.findvoice.org**

ORDER COPIES FOR YOUR SCHOOL/ORGANISATION

Brilliant Rappers Educate Intelligent Students

BREIS

Published by Student of Life Publishing

To order copies for your school or organisation send an email to studentoflife.ltd@gmail.com stating how many copies you would like, the name of your school/organisation and your postal address.
Each copy costs £5.99 plus postage.

Buy 50 copies or more and receive a 20% discount.

ACKNOWLEDGEMENTS

Thanks to Almighty God for blessing me with the inspiration and creative ability to write these lyrics. Special thanks to all the teachers who kept asking me for a book and all the students I've had the privilege of standing before to lead a workshop or perform to. You have inspired me to do this. Cover, book design and illustrations by Susan_MoreRainDesign. Thank you for all your hard work. SOL logo by Joanna Dzyna Brown. Editing by Funmi Adewale, Karen Arthur, Nii Parkes, Charlie Dark and Fiona Solomon. Special thanks to Adisa and Karl Nova. Yoruba spelling by Lanre Njoku. Marketing and PR by DWELL PR.

ENCORE - MOCKING BIRD

Thought I was over you, my triumph a hollow win

The pain following our break up, I'm swallowing

Kneeling on the ceiling with this bleeding feeling

Picture no more Mr Nice Guy killing Miss Leading

Misreading the signs, with you I'm dyslexic

Led to plotting and jotting plans for your exit

It all started with a college crush on this girl who was just

Out of a relationship but I was taught not to rush

Plus, I gave her space not in her face like dust

But now I'm sweeping up my heart cos she gave me the brush

This was after our date in a pub in Portobello

Where the ambience was mellow this fellow far from yellow

Orange moon kissing my eyes, lips caressing my flow

She let me know that she wanted to know

Then she got cold feet, we had bad timing, this man's climbing

Onto Orion, but how do you kill and bury a diamond?

Booked a cruise on a love boat and ended in a friendship
Stands to reason that I want a refund, I'm pensive
The English patient tired of ancient trends
How many times will she say, "I just wanna be friends?"
Don't drink lager but I'm bitter within cos she's with him
Didn't work out, should've gone to the gym
Feels like birds are mocking me and taking the mick
And getting over you is long, so I wrote this song
If you bury emotions alive, one day they resurrect
To erect a wreck that might cause a hazardous effect
You weren't ready for the lovin' that I govern
Now my blood's in the oven cos your words were nothing
Were you bluffing when you made me reveal
Feelings concealed, appealed to you, appealed to me; magnificent
Then your ambivalence arrived and made it tough
But I don't wanna wait in vain for your love

INSPIRATION

It's always hard when a person you like doesn't feel the same way about you. Mocking bird describes someone you thought wanted to stay with you but ends up flying away. It's something that happens to all of us at some point and time is the only medicine that helps the pain go away. The song was inspired by a college crush I once had. I was too scared to tell her that I liked her. We left college and went our separate ways. Ten years later when we met up again, I decided to tell her that I used to have a crush on her. She then told me that she used to feel the same way about me back in college (you can imagine me kicking myself when I heard that). But it's fine because it just meant that we weren't meant for each other.

Kneeling on the ceiling with this bleeding feeling Picture no more Mr Nice Guy killing Miss leading

This describes a man whose world has been turned upside down and feels that he's been misled. Miss Leading is a play on the word misleading. Wordplay is a tool I use often when writing rhymes, it's the wow factor.

END OF SHOW

MIC CHECK
Don't waste opportunities when they come around.

Notes